ACT LIKE X
Salesforce Edition

JEANETTE THEBEAU AND SARA CHOJNACKI

Copyright © 2018 by Jeanette Thebeau

All rights reserved. No portion of this book may be reproduced — mechanically, electronically, or by any other means, including photocopying — without written permission of the copyright owner and publisher.

The scanning, uploading and distribution of this book via the Internet or via any other means without the permission of the copyright owner and publisher is illegal and punishable by law.

Act Like X workbooks are available at special discounts when purchased in bulk. Special edition workbooks or workbook excerpts can also be created. For details, contact Act Like X at TellMeMore@ActLikeX.com.

Design by Jeanette Thebeau

Printed in the United States of America

Available from Amazon.com and other online stores

The information and exercises included in this workbook have not been evaluated or endorsed by Salesforce.com.

First printing August 2018

We believe every company should be true to its DNA, but to better understand what that DNA is means taking time to look at your business from a different perspective — *what's working, what's not, and what can you learn from the world's leading companies?*

Thought leads to action and action produces results. To act like a company you admire, you've got to think like one, so we've put together the Act Like X series to help you get started.

In this edition, we focus on Salesforce. It's one of those companies most of us interact with everyday, in multiple ways, without even realizing it. Retailers use Salesforce. Banks use Salesforce. Insurance companies use Salesforce. Manufacturers use Salesforce. Even charities use Salesforce. When we connect with them, we connect with Salesforce.

What we love about Salesforce is not just its intentional focus on innovation, but the way that it uses the success of its groundbreaking CRM, or "customer relationship management" software, for good. Every company is focused on growth, value and profitability, but not every company is willing to put its core values ahead of those when it has to. Salesforce walks the walk and talks the talk — and we believe there are some lessons to be learned from its approach.

We hope you get as much out of these interactive exercises as we did putting them together.

Thinking is good. Doing is better. Have fun along the way!

Jeanette and Sara

Why Act Like X?

How many times have you read a book that got you excited about a new approach and how big of an impact that could have on your company or organization? Or heard a great speaker at a conference that made you want to change the world? Or seen a thought-provoking TED Talk that inspired you to implement change... but once back in the office, dealing with the demands of the day-to-day, you just got too busy and moved on?

Act Like X is rooted in the practice of taking inspiration from others — in adopting and adapting the best practices of leading companies and executives and applying them to your own company or organization. Our workbooks and workshops are designed to help you to get informed and inspired. More importantly, they're designed to help you take action.

The exercises in this workbook are not intended to be the end-all, be-all of life and leadership at Salesforce, nor are they intended to suggest you turn your company into something it's not. They are intended to get you thinking — and doing. They are intended to get you started.

Each Act Like X workbook identifies 10 concepts you can apply from our Company-X, each one paired with an easy-to-complete exercise to get you and your team started on your quest.

Our Inspiration

We're all about looking to outside sources for ideas and inspiration. Just as this workbook has been developed as a resource for you to tap into the concepts and best practices embraced by today's boldest, most innovative, and top-performing companies, we've taken inspiration from leading authors, speakers, and organizations in creating the exercises and activities included.

In this workbook, you'll see references to Carlye Adler and Marc Benioff's, *Behind the Cloud: The Untold Story of How Salesforce.com Went from Idea to Billion-Dollar Company — and Revolutionized an Industry*; David Whitford's, *inc.com* article, "Salesforce.com: The Software and the Story"; Adam Lashinsky's, *fortune.com* story, "How CEO Marc Benioff Drives Relentless Forward Thinking at Salesforce"; and Jason Henry's, *Financial Times* feature, "Marc Benioff: taking on Silicon Valley's noxious culture" as well as concepts by Al Ries and Jack Trout, and exercises inspired by *hbr.org*, *The Business Journals* ((bizjournals.com) and *esoftskills.com*.

Who Should Act Like X?

Act Like X workbooks are great for anyone looking to explore and apply the best practices of the world's leading companies to their own company or organization. From C-Suite executives to entrepreneurs, and functional team leaders to business unit managers, Act Like X provides actionable exercises to help both individuals and teams move beyond thinking to start doing.

When, Where and How to Act Like X

Workbooks are developed to provide flexibility of use, making Act Like X ideal for interactive workshop participation at conferences and industry seminars, leadership off-sites, planning sessions and company meetings.

- Complete the exercises in sequence, or in random order based on your company's specific objectives and priorities.

- Incorporate Act Like X as an interactive element to your conference or event agenda.

- Use Act Like X in combination with recommended reading as part of a company educational module or ongoing leadership training initiative.

- Complete an exercise-a-week as part of regular team meetings.

- Plan an off-site around an Act Like X theme, or incorporate Act Like X as a component to a multi-day retreat.

Contact us to facilitate an Act Like X session and / or customize an Act Like X workbook for your company or organization.

How to Use This Workbook

 Participants

All exercises include activities for individuals to complete on their own, as well as instructions for adapting exercises and / or adding group discussion and collaboration. Recommendations for number of group participants are included for each exercise. In settings with a large number of participants, it is recommended that the team or audience be split into multiple subgroups (generally of 10 or fewer participants).

★ **Bonus Activity(ies)**

Each Act Like X concept includes a Bonus Activity(ies) for those wanting to take the idea or principle further and apply it in more depth.

 Timing

All exercises include recommended timing, and range from short (20-30 minutes) to more in-depth activities (45 minutes or longer). Most exercises can be completed in the time recommended, however, some activities may require pre-work and / or benefit from additional time spent to dive deeper (e.g. Create Alignment Through Simplicity).

1 **Sections**

Exercises are broken down into multiple sections with timing recommendations identified for each section, or group of sections. Sections can be completed in a single session or over multiple sessions, however, it is recommend that sections always be completed in sequential order.

✏️ **What You'll Need**

Each exercise includes a list of recommended materials or resources for completion of the activity. In most cases, the only materials required are the workbook and a writing utensil. For group work, flip charts or white boards and markers are also often recommended for discussion and collaboration.

Act Like X: Salesforce Edition

Since founding Salesforce.com nearly two decades ago, Marc Benioff has shepherded the company from startup to world leader, and in the process, defined what it means to be a CEO in the 21st Century.

We've focused this edition of Act Like X on Salesforce, drawing lessons, insights and best practices from books and articles written about the company, including Benioff's own bestseller, *Behind the Cloud: The Untold Story of How Salesforce.com Went from Idea to Billion-Dollar Company — and Revolutionized an Industry.*

From **Create a Culture of Inclusion and Giving** to **Position Yourself**, and **Express Gratitude and Give Praise** to **Create Alignment Through Simplicity**, the concepts have a common thread — be intentional, be innovative and be a force for good. Get started now to act like Salesforce.

Embrace the Art of Storytelling	6
Don't Let Business Become Personal	10
Position Yourself	12
Adapt and Adopt from Those You Admire	16
Create Alignment Through Simplicity	20
View Challenges As Opportunities	22
Create a Culture of Inclusion and Giving	26
Abandon That Which No Longer Serves You	30
Act As If	32
Express Gratitude and Give Praise	36

EMBRACE THE ART OF STORYTELLING

Salesforce places enormous focus on storytelling. From the company's early "End of Software" messaging to employee interactions with customers and prospects, and to their interactions with each other… the story is at the center of it all.

David Whitford covers a Salesforce.com bootcamp for new staff members in his *Inc.com* article "Salesforce.com: The Software and the Story," reporting on an early training exercise in which staff members are asked to construct a personal timeline and tell their own stories.

Why?

Because **"stories — personal stories, company stories, customer success stories — are powerful tools. They reach customers in ways that detailed offers and explanations can't."** Salesforce employees are encouraged to "weave their past experience into their journey at Salesforce," to tell their stories, and listen to and learn from the stories of others.

QUESTIONS
- How important is storytelling to you / your company?
- What's your story (personal and company)?
- When was the last time you shared your personal story with others?
- When was the last time you shared your company story with others?
- How often do you share your personal and company stories?
- When was the last time you heard a customer story and shared it?

What story are you trying to tell?

INDIVIDUAL
Imagine your personal or company story written as a movie, book or tv series and follow the instructions to identify your main characters, key events and overarching theme of your story. Give your movie, book or tv series a title, and write a movie trailer, book synopsis or tv show promo capturing your story highlights.

GROUP (2 to 6)
Groups of six or fewer, work together to write your company or organization story as a book, movie or tv series. Identify main characters, key events and milestones, and themes through your title and overview.

BONUS ACTIVITY(IES) ★
Use the note pages in back to design a movie poster, book cover or tv show banner. Organize a storytelling session at your company and share your stories.

EXERCISE
Write your story as a movie, book or tv show.

 WHAT YOU'LL NEED — *Act Like X Workbook and writing utensil; GROUPS add flip chart or white board and markers for collaboration*

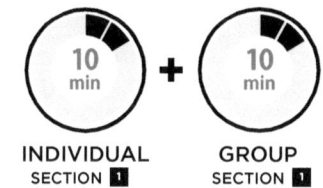

INDIVIDUAL SECTION 1   **GROUP** SECTION 1

1 Select a movie, book or tv show genre from the list below to write your personal or your company story. Groups: work together to select a genre.

- Action
- Adventure
- Comedy
- Crime
- Drama
- History
- Horror
- Family
- Musical
- Thriller
- Sci-Fi
- War
- Western
- Mystery
- Superhero
- Fantasy
- Romance
- Animation
- Sports
- Biography
- Documentary

- Tragedy
- Fantasy
- Mythology
- Action
- Adventure
- Romance
- Mystery
- Sci-Fi
- Satire
- Tragic Comedy
- Drama
- Horror
- Anthology
- Poetry
- Comics
- Series or Trilogy
- Biography
- Autobiography

- Action
- Adventure
- Sit-Com
- Crime
- Drama
- History
- Family
- Musical
- Thriller
- Sci-Fi
- News / Talk
- Western
- Mystery
- Reality TV
- Superhero
- Fantasy
- Romance
- Animation
- Sports
- Biography
- Game Show

ACT LIKE X: Salesforce Edition   7

EXERCISE
Write your story as a movie, book or tv show.

 WHAT YOU'LL NEED — *Act Like X Workbook and writing utensil; GROUPS add flip chart or white board and markers for collaboration*

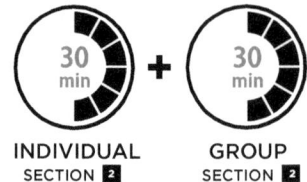

INDIVIDUAL SECTION 2 + **GROUP** SECTION 2

2 Give your movie, book or tv show a title and use the space below to list and describe the main characters. Groups: work together to create a title and identify main characters. *How do the main characters drive your story?*

EXERCISE
Write your story as a movie, book or tv show.

 WHAT YOU'LL NEED — *Act Like X Workbook and writing utensil; GROUPS add flip chart or white board and markers for collaboration*

INDIVIDUAL SECTION 3 + **GROUP** SECTION 3

3 Write a movie trailer, book synopsis or tv show promo. Groups: work together to write describe your movie, book or tv show. *What key events and interactions drive your story?*

ACT LIKE X: Salesforce Edition

DON'T LET BUSINESS BECOME PERSONAL

From its very beginning, Salesforce approached its competition head-on, in large part a dictate of its anti-software positioning. The company engaged the then market leader, Siebel, with attack ads calling out the competitor's flaws, and an aggressive grass roots strategy aimed at drawing customers away from Siebel events to learn more about Salesforce.com.

Benioff refers to a Japanese lesson he applies while engaging the competition in his book, *Behind the Cloud*, **"There is a Japanese belief that business is temporal, whereas relationships are eternal. That's true. One day you compete. The next day you partner. One day someone is your subordinate; the next day he or she may be your superior. At its finest, business is friendly competition, just like a game of tennis."**

He continues, offering the following advice: "Emotional reactions put the company at a disadvantage. Don't ever let the competition make you angry. You must have clarity of mind to make your own decisions — not the ones your competitors want you to make."

QUESTIONS
- Do you view business as friendly competition, or do you tend to take everything personally?
- Do you make decisions based on emotions, or on fact?
- How personally do you view / take internal competition (for rank / position, to win a project, etc.)?
- How personally do you view / take external competition?

Do you take things personally in the workplace?

INDIVIDUAL

Reflect on a past situation in which you took things personally. Then assess your response against the potential connections suggested by *AgileLeanLife.com* in "The proven way to stop taking things personally" to determine opportunities to work toward taking things less personally in the future.

GROUP (2 to 6)

Complete the exercise in two parts, first as individuals following the instructions above. Then, in groups of six or fewer, discuss personal challenges and support each other in setting goals.

BONUS ACTIVITY(IES)

Binge watch the AMC series *Halt and Catch Fire*, and consider the concept "business is temporal, relationships are eternal" as it relates to the characters.

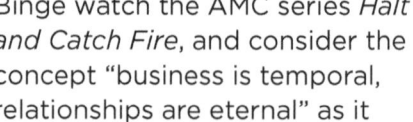

EXERCISE
Identify opportunities to stop taking things personally.

 WHAT YOU'LL NEED — *Act Like X Workbook and writing utensil*

INDIVIDUAL SECTIONS 1 2 + **GROUP** SECTIONS 1 2

1 Consider a situation when you took things personally, and — imaging yourself in the situation now — assess your reaction 1-5 (1 = completely untrue, 2 = mostly untrue, 3 = neither true or untrue, 4 = mostly true, 5 = completely true) against the statements below. Be as objective as possible.

What the other party is saying is true, but I don't want to acknowledge it.	1	2	3	4	5
What the other party is saying is true and I know it, because I follow the "fake it until you make it" philosophy and I am a work-in-progress.	1	2	3	4	5
What the other party is saying is not true but I'm not self-confident enough to ignore it.	1	2	3	4	5
My emotional response is not proportional to the issue or critique (Ask yourself, *Will I still care about this a year from now?* to determine if it is truly important.)	1	2	3	4	5
The situation brings up old feelings or reminds me of something that happened in my youth.	1	2	3	4	5
I reacted quickly without taking time to assess the situation.	1	2	3	4	5
There is a clash of interests or values between myself and the other party.	1	2	3	4	5
There is bad communication between myself and the other party.	1	2	3	4	5
The other party was merely seeking clarification and I took it personally.	1	2	3	4	5
The other party is just a hater, and despite knowing that, I let them get to me.	1	2	3	4	5
I feel excluded or out-of-place in the situation.	1	2	3	4	5
I expected others to "read my mind" and to know what I expect without telling them, and I feel hurt that they didn't deliver or live up to my expectations.	1	2	3	4	5

2 Note your 4's and 5's above and star potential solutions below offered in "The proven ways to stop taking things personally" from *AgileLeanLife.com* to take things less personally moving forward. Groups: complete individually, then discuss.

Deep down, you agree with the critique. — Make a list of arguments for why you don't agree with the statement. If a critique is justified and it hurts you, ask for clarification and make a battle plan for how you will improve yourself. Keep the growth mindset no matter how harsh the critique is.

You respond out of emotion or experience an emotional flashback. — Ask yourself about the proportion of your response to the critique and what the critique reminds you of. Analyze whether there may be an emotional flashback involved.

You perceive being treated unfairly in the situation. — Analyze how many critiques other public figures receive and realize that there is no unfairness happening to you, it's just life. Not all people can agree with you and love you.

You feel excluded. — Find a group where you really fit in and where you can blossom. Don't try to fit in with people who simply don't resonate with you.

You have unrealistic expectations. — Have realistic expectations towards people. We may be civilized animals, but none of us is perfect. Sooner or later, the people you love will hurt you and you will hurt others.

POSITION YOURSELF

The concept of positioning and differentiation has been around since the early 1970's when it was developed and introduced by Al Ries and Jack Trout.

While most companies engage in some form of positioning when developing their brands, few approach it with the fervor in which Marc Benioff did in introducing salesforce.com.

Salesforce aggressively positioned its product as an anti-software solution, calling for the "End of Software" as we knew it with a NO SOFTWARE logo. It was a bold approach, and as Benioff notes in his book, *Behind the Cloud,* "Although I loved NO SOFTWARE immediately, almost everyone else hated it... as 'it violates the number one rule of marketing: never promote yourself with a negative message'... and, 'it's not accurate, you still make software, you just deliver it differently.' "

Despite pushback, Salesforce committed to the position, and ultimately spun it into something much bigger than a new product offering — the introduction of an entirely new industry: Software-as-a-Service (SaaS).

QUESTIONS
- Can you communicate your product or brand positioning in a single sentence?
- Can other members of your team communicate it?
- How well is your product or service differentiated from the competition?
- Is your product or brand positioning claim believable to your customer or user-base?
- Is your positioning relevant to your target customers?

Do you have a strong position in the marketplace?

INDIVIDUAL

Thinking of positioning, not as how you see yourself but how others see you, capture your company's existing position in the marketplace. Then develop your company's ideal position (how you would like others to see you) and evaluate it through a series of key questions and filters.

GROUP 2 to 10

Complete the exercise in two parts, first as individuals following the instructions above. Then, in groups of 10 or fewer, compare the ideal positions developed and collaborate to develop a unified ownable, believable and relevant position for your company.

BONUS ACTIVITY(IES) ★

Review all company touch points against your ideal position. *Are external (customer-facing) activities aligned with the position you would like to occupy in the mind of your customers and prospects?*

EXERCISE
Develop and evaluate your position in the marketplace.

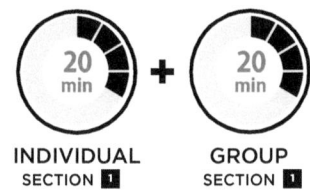

WHAT YOU'LL NEED — *Act Like X Workbook and writing utensil; GROUPS add flip chart or white board and markers for collaboration*

 Consider the quotes below from Ries and Trout, and Jeff Bezos, and answer the Six Questions to Ask When Positioning Your Business from *Positioning: The Battle for Your Mind* by Al Ries and Jack Trout. Groups: complete individually, then discuss.

"Positioning is not what you do to a product. It's what you do to the mind of the prospect." — Al Ries and Jack Trout

"Your brand (positioning) is what other people say about you when you're not in the room." — Jeff Bezos

---

POSITIONING YOUR BUSINESS — The Six Questions to Ask

1. **What position do you (currently) own?** *Positioning is thinking in reverse. Instead of starting with yourself, you start with the mind of the prospect.*

2. **What position do you want to own?** *This is where you bring out your crystal ball and try to figure out the best position to own from a long-term point-of-view. "Own" is the key word.*

3. **Whom must you outgun?** *Try to select a position that no one else has a firm grip on.*

4. **Do you have enough money (to own it)?** *A big obstacle to successful positioning is attempting to achieve the impossible. It takes money to build share-of-mind. It takes money to establish a position. It takes money to hold a position once you've established it.*

5. **Can you stick it out?** *To cope with change, it's important to take a long-range point of view. To determine your basic position and then stick to it.*

6. **Do you match your position?** *Does your messaging match your position?*

EXERCISE
Develop and evaluate your position in the marketplace.

✏ **WHAT YOU'LL NEED —** *Act Like X Workbook and writing utensil; GROUPS add flip chart or white board and markers for collaboration*

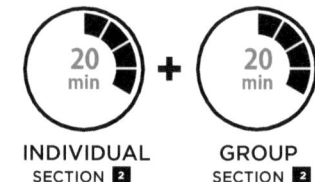

INDIVIDUAL SECTION 2 + **GROUP** SECTION 2

2 Consider your responses to the Six Questions to Ask When Positioning Your Business on the previous page, and answer the Three W's and an H below to clearly articulate the position you own or would like to own in the marketplace. Groups: complete individually, then discuss.

WHAT DO YOU DO?

HOW DO YOU DO IT?

WHY DOES IT MATTER?

WHO CARES?

14 ACT LIKE X: Salesforce Edition

EXERCISE
Develop and evaluate your position in the marketplace.

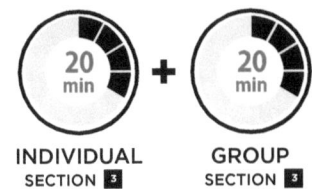

INDIVIDUAL SECTION 3 + **GROUP** SECTION 3

 WHAT YOU'LL NEED — *Act Like X Workbook and writing utensil;* GROUPS add flip chart or white board and markers for collaboration

3 Evaluate your position or desired position using the ownable / believable / relevant framework below. Groups: complete individually, then discuss. *Does your position meet all criteria to fall within the overlapping area (asterisk) of the Venn diagram?*

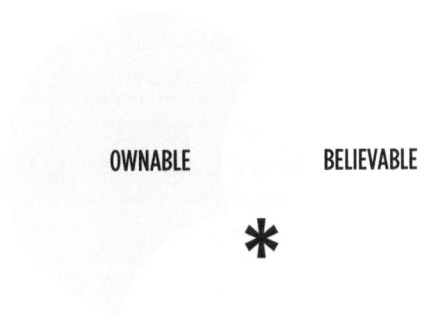

OWNABLE — context: competition
Consider your answers to the questions **What do you do?** and **How do you do it?** on the previous page. Is what you do and how you do it differentiated from your competition?

BELIEVABLE — context: yourself / your company
Can you or your company deliver on the ownable position as described?

RELEVANT — context: target customer or user
Consider your answers to the questions **Why does it matter?** and **Who cares?** on the previous page. Is what you do and how you do it relevant? Is it relevant to a significant enough target audience to make it a viable position?

OWNABLE — context: competition
Is your position or desired position truly ownable?
If not, what (if anything) can you do to make it ownable?

BELIEVABLE — context: your company
Can you truly deliver on the position as described?
If not, what (if anything) can you do to make it believable?

RELEVANT — context: target customer
Is your position truly relevant as described?
If not, what (if anything) can you do to make it relevant?

ACT LIKE X: Salesforce Edition

ADAPT AND ADOPT FROM THOSE YOU ADMIRE

Marc Benioff and Salesforce.com have been "acting like X" for years, taking inspiration from others to create products, set priorities and develop leadership principles.

In a 2017 interview with Adam Lashinsky for *fortune.com*, Benioff "pays homage to Amazon, an early inspiration for the type of consumer experience Salesforce aims to deliver. He unabashedly notes that Salesforce's earliest versions were copies of Amazon's user interface... because they are not training anybody to use their website, and we want to build software that's not going to be like the current generation of enterprise software."

"Benioff credits a diverse set of influences. From (Klaus) Schwab, he took the concept of 'stakeholders' as opposed to only shareholders. Larry Ellison, his first boss, motivated Benioff by helping him see the value of new ideas... And he has learned the value of being inquisitive from a guru of self-improvement: 'My friend Tony Robbins says the quality of your life is created by the quality of your questions.'"

QUESTIONS
- What companies or organizations and leaders do you respect and admire?
- What do they do that inspires you?
- Where can you adopt and adapt their best practices to improve your personal or company performance?
- What will it take to apply these practices to your company or organization?

Who inspires you and what can you learn from them?

INDIVIDUAL

Follow the three step process — get inspired, deconstruct, and upcycle and own — to identify opportunities to adapt and adopt best practices from companies, brands and leaders you admire.

GROUP 2 to 6

Complete the exercise in two parts, first as individuals following the instructions above. Then, in groups of six or fewer, compare inspiration lists, best practices deconstruction, and upcycle and own opportunities. Then collaborate to create a group adapt and adopt list.

BONUS ACTIVITY(IES) ★

REALLY OWN IT! Consider your upcycle and own list to create a program or initiative around one of your adapted best practices. Give the program or initiative a short and memorable name and support it with visuals.

EXERCISE
Adopt and adapt best practices to grow your business.

✏ **WHAT YOU'LL NEED —** *Act Like X Workbook and writing utensil; GROUPS add flip chart or white board and markers for collaboration*

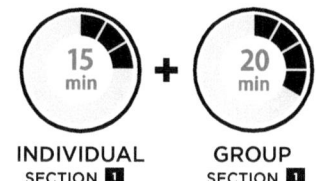

INDIVIDUAL SECTION 1   **GROUP** SECTION 1

1 Get Inspired — use the space below to make a list of companies or brands and leaders that inspire you. Groups: complete individually, then discuss.

1. GET INSPIRED:
Make a list of companies, brands and leaders that inspire you.

2. DECONSRUCT:
Review their best practices and break them down.

3. UPCYCLE & OWN
Add, delete, and adapt best practices to make them your own.

GET INSPIRED

ACT LIKE X: Salesforce Edition

EXERCISE
Adopt and adapt best practices to grow your business.

 WHAT YOU'LL NEED — *Act Like X Workbook and writing utensil; GROUPS add flip chart or white board and markers for collaboration*

INDIVIDUAL SECTION 2 + **GROUP** SECTION 2

2 Deconstruct — consider the list of those you admire on the previous page and deconstruct their best practices. *What do they do that works? How does it work? How SPECIFICALLY does it work?* Groups: complete individually, then discuss.

1. GET INSPIRED:
Make a list of companies, brands and leaders that inspire you.

2. DECONSRUCT:
Review their best practices and break them down.

3. UPCYCLE & OWN
Add, delete, and adapt best practices to make them your own.

DECONSTRUCT

EXERCISE
Adopt and adapt best practices to grow your business.

 WHAT YOU'LL NEED — *Act Like X Workbook and writing utensil; GROUPS add flip chart or white board and markers for collaboration*

INDIVIDUAL SECTION 3 **GROUP** SECTION 3

3 Upcycle & Own — review your list of deconstructed best practice elements and make three lists, identifying: 1) those elements which you would like to adopt and integrate; 2) those which do not fit with your company and you would like to discard; and 3) those which can be customized and adapted to fit your company in some way. Groups: complete individually, then discuss.

 **1. GET INSPIRED:** Make a list of companies, brands and leaders that inspire you.

 **2. DECONSRUCT:** Review their best practices and break them down.

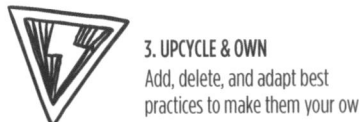 **3. UPCYCLE & OWN** Add, delete, and adapt best practices to make them your own.

UPCYCLE & OWN

ACT LIKE X: Salesforce Edition

CREATE ALIGNMENT THROUGH SIMPLICITY

Strategic planning takes many forms, with companies and organizations implementing KPIs, rocks, blue chips, MBOs, etc. as a framework to manage business goals and objectives, and provide a reference for personal accountability.

Salesforce.com found many of these programs were "difficult to digest and take longer to understand than they do to implement." What's more, "the metrics are stagnant, and they don't work in today's fast-moving environment, which requires that companies adapt continuously," explains Benioff in his book, *Behind the Cloud*.

His solution? A framework he developed to offer "a new simplicity," and referred to as V2MOM.

"V2MOM is an acronym that stands for visions, values, methods, obstacles and measures... it is a living document, rewritten every six months, shared with top officers for feedback, and cascaded and communicated to the entire company. And we now collaborate on the corporate V2MOM with all employees through our IdeaExchange, a social networking tool that employees use to contribute ideas and promote and comment on others' ideas."

QUESTIONS
- What planning framework is your company or organization currently using?
- How effective is it in managing your business goals and objectives?
- Is everyone on the team aligned with the company vision?
- Does everyone understand their role in achieving company goals and objectives?

How aligned is your team on company vision?

INDIVIDUAL

Follow the instruction to use Marc Benioff and Salesforce's planning framework, and create a V2MOM for your company.

GROUP 2 to 10

Complete the exercise in two parts, first as individuals following the instructions above. Then, in groups of ten or fewer who work together, compare — *How similar or different are your V2MOMs?* — and collaborate to create a group V2MOM for your company.

BONUS ACTIVITY(IES) ★

Look for opportunities to cascade your V2MOM throughout your company or organization.

Ask each executive to create his or her own V2MOM — and then have direct reports create their own and so on.

Use V2MOMs as a basis for performance reviews.

EXERCISE
Use Benioff's framework to create your company vision.

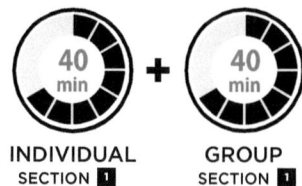

INDIVIDUAL SECTION 1 + **GROUP** SECTION 1

 WHAT YOU'LL NEED — *Act Like X Workbook and writing utensil;* GROUPS *add flip chart or white board and markers for collaboration*

1 Follow Benioff's framework and answer the questions below to create a V2MOM for your company, or follow the instruction on ADOPT AND ADAPT FROM THOSE YOU ADMIRE to customize the V2MOM framework to fit your needs. Groups: complete individually, then compare and collaborate to create a joint company V2MOM.

VISION — What do you want?

VALUES — What's important about it?

METHODS — How do you get it?

OBSTACLES — What might stand in the way?

MEASURE — How will you know when you have it?

ACT LIKE X: Salesforce Edition   21

VIEW CHALLENGES AS OPPORTUNITIES

Benioff calls this lesson out in his book, *Behind the Cloud*, priding the Salesforce team on being prepared for anything and everything to happen, offering an example of his team's ability to pivot and make the most of circumstances outside the control of the company...

Salesforce's annual Dreamforce conference was scheduled to kick off on Election Day in 2004. As Benioff notes, "It wasn't an ideal time to hold a conference, but it was the Hilton San Francisco's only available time.

"Two weeks before the conference, all San Francisco hotel employees went on strike." Rather than panic, the Salesforce team jumped in creating plans for every scenario, including multiple versions of messaging and staffing, last-minute booking of a new location for the keynote address, and the addition of a George W. Bush Election Day comedy sketch.

The conference was a huge success, in large part because the Salesforce team had fun with the challenge, "turning what others may have seen as a hardship into an opportunity to create something great."

QUESTIONS
- How well do you respond and adapt to changes in circumstances outside your control?
- How does your company react to surprises in the marketplace?
- Does your company / team panic or get busy (and creative) finding solutions when challenges arise?

How well do you respond to and "spin" challenges?

INDIVIDUAL
Follow the instructions to create a fictitious challenging scenario related to a real company project or initiative. Then identify constraints and resources available to you to turn the challenge into an opportunity and brainstorm.

GROUP (2 to 6)
Complete the exercise in two parts, first as individuals following the instructions above. Then, in groups of six or fewer, compare and collaborate to brainstorm solutions turning challenges into opportunities.

BONUS ACTIVITY(IES) ★
Review your company or department SWOT, and identify threats you can prepare for in advance. Write a Worst Case Scenario Survival Handbook for your company including plans to address anticipated threats or challenges.

EXERCISE
Get creative to turn unforeseen challenges into opportunities.

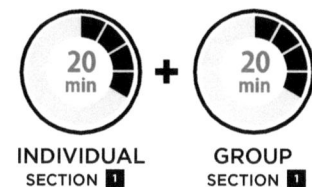

INDIVIDUAL SECTION 1

GROUP SECTION 1

 WHAT YOU'LL NEED — *Act Like X Workbook and writing utensil; GROUPS add flip chart or white board and markers for collaboration*

1 Thinking about a current project or initiative, imagine getting the call you don't want to get with the news you don't want to hear about circumstances outside your control resulting in something significant not going according to plan. Groups: complete individually, then discuss.

Use the speech bubbles to identify three different sets of challenging circumstances related to your project or initiative, and **write in what you are hearing from the person on the other end of the line.**

Sorry to have to tell you this, but...

You're not going to want to hear this, but...

I have some bad news about...

ACT LIKE X: Salesforce Edition

EXERCISE
Get creative to turn unforeseen challenges into opportunities.

INDIVIDUAL SECTION 2
GROUP SECTION 2

✏ **WHAT YOU'LL NEED** — *Act Like X Workbook and writing utensil; GROUPS add flip chart or white board and markers for collaboration*

 Select one imagined challenging scenario related to your project or initiative from the previous page, and consider the constraints to turning the situation into an opportunity. Once complete, put a star next to those things that are not constraints and / or things you are empowered to change, and put an X next to constraints. Groups: complete individually, then discuss.

1. **Are there any constraints related to budget you should consider?** *What are they? Are you empowered to spend whatever is necessary to address the challenge and turn it into an opportunity?*

2. **Are there any constraints related to timing you should consider?** *What are they? Are you empowered to alter the project or initiative timeline to address the challenge and turn it into an opportunity?*

3. **Are there any constraints related to personnel / people resources you should consider?** *What human resources do you have available to address the challenge and turn it into an opportunity? Who can you recruit to your team that thinks outside the box to find solutions to difficult situations? If time is a constraint, who can you recruit to your team to gets things done quickly and without error?*

4. **Are there any constraints related to location or geography you should consider?** *What are they? Are you empowered to make changes to the project or initiative location or geography to address the challenge and turn it into an opportunity?*

5. **Are there any constraints related to marketing or promotion you should consider?** *What are they? Are you empowered to change the project or initiative marketing to address the challenge and turn it into an opportunity?*

6. **Are there any other constraints you should consider?** *What are they?*

EXERCISE
Get creative to turn unforeseen challenges into opportunities.

 WHAT YOU'LL NEED — *Act Like X Workbook, writing utensil and highlighter*
GROUPS add flip chart or white board and markers for collaboration

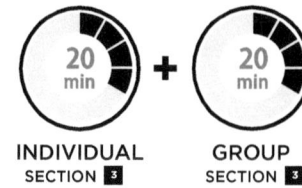

INDIVIDUAL   **GROUP**
SECTION 3   SECTION 3

3   Consider your lists of constraints, and things you are empowered to change / resources you have to work with, and use the space below to ideate turning your challenging scenario into an opportunity. If you feel stuck, ask others to ideate with you. Groups: complete individually, then discuss and collaborate. Check out IDEO's 7 Rules of Brainstorming below to optimize your ideation.

★ **Is there anything about your project or initiative you wanted to change pre-challenge?** *Do you have an opportunity to change it now as part of your plan to turn your challenging scenario into an opportunity?*

IDEO'S 7 RULES OF BRAINSTORMING:
1. Defer Judgment
2. Encourage Wild Ideas
3. Be Visual
4. Build on the Ideas of Others
5. One Conversation at a Time
6. Stay on Topic
7. Go for Quantity of Ideas

ACT LIKE X: Salesforce Edition

CREATE A CULTURE OF INCLUSION AND GIVING

Culture has gained importance over the past decade, as a means to create coherence between companies and their employees, attract and retain better talent, and amplify brand identity.

Salesforce not only embraces its significance, but takes it a step further, amplifying its benefits by continually working to **create a culture of inclusion and giving back**.

Consider the following, as reported by Jason Henry in his January 2018 *Financial Times* article, "Marc Benioff: taking on Silicon Valley's noxious culture:"

- The Salesforce.com headquarters "Ohana" floor, which means "family" in Hawaiian — used as a company-wide hang-out space and as a venue for after-hours nonprofits use
- Salesforce is among the most diverse of the Big Tech companies — 35% of employees are minorities
- The company's lauded and much copied 1-1-1 model — in which it donates 1% of equity, 1% of employee time, and 1% of products to nonprofits
- Benioff's tweet threatening to pull jobs out of Indiana following the introduction of legislation that discriminated against the LGBT community "because it's what our employees demanded."

QUESTIONS
- How well-defined is your company culture?
- Is your culture strong, unified and easy to articulate?
- Is yours a culture of inclusion or exclusion?
- Is yours a culture of giving back?
- As leadership, what changes would you like to make to improve your company culture?

Is yours a culture of inclusion and giving?

INDIVIDUAL

Review your company culture against the "Six Components of a Great Culture" from *hbr.org*, and identify opportunities to create a culture of inclusion and giving. Then, create a culture formula for your company or organization, highlighting components which support inclusion and giving within your company.

GROUP 2 to 6

Complete the exercise in two parts, first as individuals following the instructions above. Then, in groups of six or fewer, compare — *How similar or different are your assessments?* — and collaborate to create a group culture formula.

BONUS ACTIVITY(IES) ★

Create a calendar of company activities and initiatives supporting the concepts of inclusion and giving to continue to assess your efforts and ensure activation around these themes.

EXERCISE
Identify opportunities to create a culture of inclusion and giving.

 WHAT YOU'LL NEED — *Act Like X Workbook and writing utensil;* GROUPS add flip chart or white board and markers for collaboration

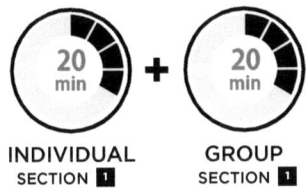

INDIVIDUAL SECTION 1 + **GROUP** SECTION 1

1 Consider the "Six Components of a Great (Company) Culture" from *hbr.org* and use adjectives to describe the elements of your company's culture today (current) and as you would like it to be (aspirational). Then, circle the adjectives that support, and place an "X" next to those that create barriers to inclusion and giving. Groups: complete individually, then discuss.

	CURRENT CULTURE	ASPIRATIONAL CULTURE
Vision — A great culture starts with a vision or mission statement. These simple turns of phrase guide a company's values and provide it with purpose. That purpose, in turn, orients every decision employees make.		
Values — A company's values are the core of its culture. While a vision articulates a company's purpose, values offer a set of guidelines on the behaviors and mindsets needed to achieve that vision.		
Practices — Whatever an organization's values, they must be reinforced in review criteria and promotion policies, and baked into the operating principles of daily life in the firm.		
People — No company can build a coherent culture without people who either share its core values or possess the willingness and ability to embrace those values. That's why the greatest firms in the world also have some of the most stringent recruiting policies.		

EXERCISE
Identify opportunities to create a culture of inclusion and giving.

✏ **WHAT YOU'LL NEED —** *Act Like X Workbook and writing utensil;*
GROUPS add flip chart or white board and markers for collaboration

  CONTINUED — Consider the "Six Components of a Great (Company) Culture" from *hbr.org* and use adjectives to describe the elements of your company's culture today (current) and as you would like it to be (aspirational). Then, circle the adjectives that support, and place an "X" next to those that create barriers to inclusion and giving. Groups: complete individually, then discuss.

	CURRENT CULTURE	ASPIRATIONAL CULTURE
Narrative Every organization has a unique history, and the ability to draft that history into a narrative is a core element of culture creation. The elements of the company narrative can be formal — like Coca-Cola's focus on celebrating its heritage — or informal, like stories about how Jobs' early fascination with calligraphy shaped Apple's aesthetically-oriented culture.		
Place Place shapes culture. Open architecture is more conducive to certain office behaviors, like collaboration. Certain cities and countries have local cultures that may reinforce or contradict the culture a firm is trying to create. Place — whether geography, architecture, or aesthetic design — impacts the values and behaviors of people in a workplace.		

How does your self-described current culture compare to your aspirational culture?
- How large are the gaps?
- What can you do to create your aspirational culture NOW?
- What can you plan for to create your aspirational culture in the FUTURE?

EXERCISE
Identify opportunities to create a culture of inclusion and giving.

 WHAT YOU'LL NEED — *Act Like X Workbook and writing utensil; GROUPS add flip chart or white board and markers for collaboration*

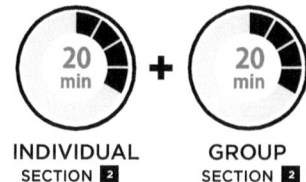

INDIVIDUAL SECTION 2   **GROUP** SECTION 2

2 Consider the sample culture formula created by a software development firm below, and use the adjectives identified on the previous two pages to think outside the box and create a formula for your aspirational company culture. Focus on components that support inclusion and giving. Groups: complete individually, then discuss opportunities to bring the formula to life.

SAMPLE CULTURE FORMULA — Software Company X = Pe x Pl x Va x Re

Pe = (C + O + P)Q + Ch(CTW + PoC + F)
Pl = (CS + WB + DEM)/nTM x (h(PP + Po) + n(D + OP) x AHF
Va = ((Cr + VL + I) x RWE)/Df
Re = (S + PSh + Eq) x Ex x PS

People = (Curiosity + Optimism + Passion) Quotient + Character (Change-the-World + Perfecting our Craft + Fun)

Place = (Collaboration Spaces + Whiteboards + Dry Erase Markers)/number of Team Members x ((hours(Ping Pong + Pool) + number (Dogs + Other Pets)) x After-Hours Fun

Values = ((Craftsmanship + Validated Learning + Iteration) x Real-World Experience)/Defects

Reward = (Salary + Profit Sharing + Equity) x Experience x Personal Satisfaction

ABANDON THAT WHICH NO LONGER SERVES YOU

Embracing the edict of self-help guru Tony Robbins — "Stay committed to your decisions, but stay flexible in your approach. It's the end you're after." — Salesforce is resolute in its "No Sacred Cows" declaration and its willingness to change direction to grow and succeed.

As Benioff writes in *Behind the Cloud*, "As we grew distribution, we soon discovered that some of the strategies that had proven successful in the past no longer made sense as we evolved."

By continually challenging their existing way of doing things, the leadership team at Salesforce has been able to quickly and successfully adapt and pivot when necessary, abandoning the old in favor of new strategies on everything from marketing and lead-generation to pricing models.

Marc's advice?

"Keep in mind that the landscape is always changing; you must always examine what's working, evolve your ideas, and change the way you do things."

QUESTIONS
- How change-averse is your company or organization?
- How change-averse are you personally?
- When was the last time you heard an employee at your company say they were approaching a problem in a certain way because "that's the way we've always done it?"
- Have you ever been that employee?
- Have you ever copied and pasted last year's strategy into this year's plan?

How flexible and adaptable are you in the workplace?

INDIVIDUAL

Assess your flexibility and adaptability skills using the the "Tips for Being More Flexible and Adaptable" from *The Business Journals* and *esoftskills.com,* and identify opportunities to be more flexible moving forward. Consider your own "sacred cows" and ask yourself if you adhere to them because they are the best approach, or because they are "the way you've always done things."

GROUP (2 to 6)

Complete the exercise in two parts, first as individuals following the instructions above. Then, in groups of six or fewer who work together, discuss opportunities to be more flexible and adaptable as a team.

BONUS ACTIVITY(IES)

Make a list of your company's "sacred cows" and challenge them.

EXERCISE
Rate yourself flexibility and adaptability themes.

 WHAT YOU'LL NEED — *Act Like X Workbook and writing utensil*

INDIVIDUAL SECTION **1** **GROUP** SECTION **1**

1 Consider the following "Tips for Being More Flexible and Adaptable" from *The Business Journals* and esoftskills.com and rate your actions in adapting to change in the workplace 1-5 (1 = never, 2 = rarely, 3 = sometimes, 4 = mostly, 5 = always). Be as objective as possible. *What do you need to do to earn more 4's and 5's?* Groups: complete individually, then discuss.

Embrace Ambiguity — Encourage an environment where change is embraced, even when ambiguity is involved. Make a conscious effort to come up with new ways of seeing and doing things.	1	2	3	4	5
Consider the Bigger Picture — It's like watching a hockey game: if you follow the puck with your eyes, you'll be lost. If you zoom out and look at the patterns of the players on the ice, you'll see the whole game. Zoom out and look for patterns.	1	2	3	4	5
Really Listen — When you listen, you're suspending judgement. You're taking in information that will allow you to select the best response to the situation (not just the one you've always gone with).	1	2	3	4	5
Implement Team Problem-Solving Measures — Meet with key staff members when issues arise. Solicit insights and solutions from your team vs. making the call yourself.	1	2	3	4	5
Think Creatively — Encourage exploration of different avenues for fostering creativity and accomplishing work goals with a new mindset. Those who tend to stick to the same tried-and-true methods are likely to have decreased flexibility and will resist change.	1	2	3	4	5
Suggest Positive Aspects of a Challenging Situation — Resist insisting that change cannot work; instead look for the opportunity to try a new approach. Advocate for the "silver lining" in each situation.	1	2	3	4	5
Accept Multiple Perspectives — We often think we have taken a wide variety of perspectives into consideration, when really we have mostly asked the people whose ideas we already know about. The key to seeking out different perspectives is not trying to convince anyone (especially ourselves) that we're right.	1	2	3	4	5
Keep Calm in the Face of Change — Take a deep breath. Panic tends to direct behavior toward the safest option. Whenever possible, take the emotional steam out of a decision by calming the amygdala, the part of the brain that runs on instinct, impulse and raw emotion (such as fear).	1	2	3	4	5
Don't Rush to Form an Opinion — Try holding back on forming an opinion until you've considered multiple approaches, and keep asking yourself "In what ways could I be wrong or missing something?"	1	2	3	4	5
Shift Focus — Continually reset your focus in accordance with your organization's changing priorities. Maintaining focus on operational goals — while using creative and critical thinking processes to solve problems — is key to creating a dynamic environment.	1	2	3	4	5

ACT AS IF

Who's not familiar with the term "act as if?" It's been around since the 1920's when it was introduced by Alfred Adler, a disciple of Sigmund Freud, as a strategy to provide clients with a method to practice alternatives to dysfunctional behaviors. In fact, just typing the phrase into your google search bar with get you nearly 1.5 billion results.

"Acting as if" is about accepting your current reality, while also being willing to look beyond it. While most think of the term as a strategy for manifesting personal change, Marc Benioff and Salesforce.com embrace this concept and put it into effect at the company level, imagining where the organization would like to be, and acting as if their goals have already been met.

In his book, *Behind the Cloud*, Benioff gives an example of acting as if: "Years ago, we received criticism for spending 'too much' on marketing for a $250 million company, but when we were a $250 million company, we weren't thinking like a $250 million company. We were trying to build a bigger company, and the only way to do that was to act like one."

QUESTIONS
- Is your company stuck in its current reality, taking actions which only reinforce your limitations?
- Do you accept your current marketplace reality, but look beyond it and imagine the company you want to be?
- What actions do you currently take to "act as if" you are already the company you want to be?

Are you able to "act as if" to become it?

INDIVIDUAL
Write a brand or company obituary to identify opportunities to think beyond your current company reality. Then assess your progress toward achieving your goals and look for opportunities to manifest accomplishments by "acting as if."

GROUP (2 to 6)
Complete the exercise in two parts, first as individuals following the instructions above. Then, in groups of six or fewer, compare obituary highlights and key milestones accomplished, and collaborate to create group "act as if" opportunities.

BONUS ACTIVITY(IES)
Set weekly, bi-weekly or monthly reminders to check your progress against and hold yourself accountable to "acting as if."

EXERCISE
Write your brand's obituary and determine "act as if" opportunities.

INDIVIDUAL SECTION **1** + GROUP SECTION **1**

 WHAT YOU'LL NEED — *Act Like X Workbook, writing utensil and highlighter*
GROUPS add flip chart or white board and markers for collaboration

1 Read the excerpt below from an *hbr.org* article by Denise Lee Yohn, and write an obituary for your brand or company on the following page. Groups: complete individually, then discuss.

WRITE YOUR BRAND'S OBITUARY

Excerpt below by contributor Denise Lee Yohn, author of *What Great Brands Do: The Seven Brand-Building Principles that Separate the Best from the Rest* and *FUSION: How Integrating Brand and Culture Powers the World's Greatest Companies*.

Consider, what would happen if your company ceased to exist?

Would journalists write headlines heralding your past achievements, or would their stories simply add you to a list of bygones? Would analysts express disappointment or would they point to indicators that made your death predictable? Would employees wonder how it could have ended, or would they have known it was inevitable? Would customers mourn your passing, or would the demise of your brand go unnoticed? Try this exercise: writing a Brand Obituary.

It's not the most pleasant thought, but it focuses the mind to imagine what it would be like if indeed your brand ceased to exist.

In this exercise, it helps to think of your brand as though it were a person — the type of person the brand would be if it came to life today. Think of your brand in its totality, as all that the brand entails — *and on its best days, when it's executing with excellence.*

Pretend that you are a reporter for a local newspaper who must write the obituary for this person — your brand — who just passed away today. This invented scenario can help you uncover the true nature of your brand.

Here are some questions to answer in the obituary:

- What was the brand's biggest accomplishment in life? What will it be remembered for?
- Who did the brand leave behind? What did the brand leave unaccomplished? Who will mourn or miss the brand, and why?
- What lessons can be learned from the brand's life? What can be learned in the wake of its death?
- Now that the brand is gone, what will take its place?

Once you've completed the column, write a headline to capture the essence of the obituary.

EXERCISE
Write your brand's obituary and determine "act as if" opportunities.

✏️ **WHAT YOU'LL NEED —** *Act Like X Workbook, writing utensil and highlighter*
GROUPS add flip chart or white board and markers for collaboration

 CONTINUED — Read the excerpt on the previous page from an *hbr.org* article by Denise Lee Yohn, and write an obituary for your brand or company on the following page. Groups: complete individually, then discuss.

EXERCISE
Write your brand's obituary and determine "act as if" opportunities.

✏ **WHAT YOU'LL NEED —** *Act Like X Workbook*, writing utensil and highlighter
GROUPS add flip chart or white board and markers for collaboration

INDIVIDUAL SECTIONS 2 3 + **GROUP** SECTIONS 2 3

2 Highlight the positive accomplishments called out in your brand or company obituary on the previous page. List them below and indicate if your company has or has not already achieved this milestone. Groups: complete individually, then discuss.

ACCOMPLISHMENT / MILESTONE	ACCOMPLISHED? YES / NO / IN-PROGRESS

3 Select three accomplishments above that you have NOT already achieved, and use the space below to identify up to five things you can start doing NOW to **"act as if"** you have already achieved this milestone. Groups: complete individually, then discuss.

1.

2.

3.

ACT LIKE X: Salesforce Edition   **35**

EXPRESS GRATITUDE AND GIVE PRAISE

Salesforce believes it's necessary for every company to integrate *mahalo* — the Hawaiian spirit of gratitude and praise — into its corporate culture." Benioff explains the importance of *mahalo* in his book, Behind the Cloud, "It's simple enough to reward employees for extra performance with extraordinary compensation and a competitive rewards portfolio, but **it's really the everyday environment that contributes to people's happiness, success, and longevity at a company."**

Check out a few of the ways Salesforce expresses gratitude and gives praise:

- A kitchen stocked with healthy snacks
- Massages for members of the tech team following each release
- Company-paid gym memberships and free yoga classes with a renowned instructor
- Discounted tickets on Hawaiian Airlines
- Maui trips for any salesperson who makes quota (vs. top sellers only)

In addition, Salesforce has implemented a peer-recognition program, rewarding winners with $500 bonuses... and, says Benioff, "perhaps our most unusual — and visible — award recognizes distinguished employees with a life-size poster of them, which we display throughout our office."

QUESTIONS

- Does your company embrace the concept of *mahalo* as part of your culture?
- Do you personally and does your company express gratitude for employee effort on a regular basis?
- What do you do to express gratitude and give praise to employees through "small things?"

How well do you express gratitude and give praise?

INDIVIDUAL

Think about your current personal and company efforts to express gratitude and give praise. List five individuals (or teams) who have impressed you over the past week and express gratitude and give praise to them now if you haven't already.

GROUP 2 to 6

Complete the exercise in two parts, first as individuals following the instructions above. Then, in groups of six or fewer, discuss opportunities to express (more) gratitude and give (more) praise, both individually and as a company or organization.

BONUS ACTIVITY(IES)

Create your own version of *mahalo* — a theme for your company or department that represents the act of expressing gratitude and giving praise.

EXERCISE
Start expressing gratitude and giving praise NOW.

 WHAT YOU'LL NEED — *Act Like X Workbook and writing utensil; access to customer or target customer (and incentives if necessary)*

INDIVIDUAL SECTION 1 + **GROUP** SECTION 1

1 List five people who have impressed you over the past week (these can be at any level of the organization and can include those above you, below you or peers. Include at least one person who did not impress you with a specific task or deliverable, but who impresses you day-in and day-out with their professionalism, loyalty, work ethic, attitude, etc. Groups: complete individually, then discuss.

TEAM MEMBER AND ATTRIBUTE OR TASK / ACCOMPLISHMENT THAT IMPRESSED YOU

TEAM MEMBER AND ATTRIBUTE OR TASK / ACCOMPLISHMENT THAT IMPRESSED YOU

TEAM MEMBER AND ATTRIBUTE OR TASK / ACCOMPLISHMENT THAT IMPRESSED YOU

TEAM MEMBER AND ATTRIBUTE OR TASK / ACCOMPLISHMENT THAT IMPRESSED YOU

TEAM MEMBER WHO IMPRESSES YOU DAY-IN AND DAY-OUT

INDIVIDUALS

The key to expressing gratitude and giving praise is to just do it and to start NOW. If your company has a formal program for expressing gratitude and giving praise, use it. If not, you can do it on your own.

Review your list of five individuals who have impressed your over the past week above. *Have you told them formally or informally what a great job you think they do or did?*

If you haven't, tell them right now (email, text, call, etc.). The message doesn't need to be long or involved, but should call out what he or she did to impress you and how it makes you feel, and include a note of thanks.

EXERCISE
Start expressing gratitude and giving praise NOW.

✏️ **WHAT YOU'LL NEED —** *Act Like X Workbook, writing utensil and highlighter*
GROUPS add flip chart or white board and markers for collaboration

 CONTINUED — LEADERSHIP: Thinking about your current company culture, review the questions below and identify opportunities to express (more) gratitude and give (more) praise. Groups: complete individually, then discuss.

LEADERSHIP

Does your company have a formal (digital or physical) means of giving praise and celebrating individual and team success?

How do you personally and how does your company or department express gratitude?

Do you have a budget for small perks? What are they? Who do they benefit? Are they effective?

What else can you do / offer to show your gratitude for your employees and their effort?

If your budget does not allow for you to pay for perks, who can you partner with or what partnerships do you have in place which would allow you to barter for in-kind trade-outs to be used as gratitude offerings to your team?

NOTES

> "One idea alone is a tactic, but if it can be executed a number of different ways, it becomes a great strategy."
> — Marc Benioff

> 1) Out of clutter find simplicity; 2) From discord find harmony; 3) In the middle of difficulty lies opportunity.
> — Marc Benioff

> **I strongly believe the business of a business is to improve the world.**
> — Marc Benioff

> **The only constant in the technology industry is change.**
> — Marc Benioff

> "You must always examine what's working, evolve your ideas, and change the way you do things."
> — Marc Benioff

> "What part of media doesn't need to connect with their customers more smartly?"
> — Marc Benioff

> **Reliability is a tech problem, but the way you solve it is not with technology alone — it's with communication.**
> — Marc Benioff

 I mentor a lot of CEOs and entrepreneurs, and when I see that product is the number-one thing, the only thing that matters, that's a real red flag.

— Marc Benioff

Check us out at:
www.ActLikeX.com

For more information regarding conference,
off-site and on-site workshop facilitation; or to inquire
about creation of a custom Act Like X workbook
for your conference or event, contact us at:

TellMeMore@ActLikeX.com

www.ingramcontent.com/pod-product-compliance
Lightning Source LLC
Chambersburg PA
CBHW051218220526
45473CB00003B/1087